30
to Getting Along
with Absolutely Anyone

Chuck Spezzano
PH.D

ARTHUR JAMES
EVESHAM

First published in Great Britain in 1996 by

ARTHUR JAMES LTD
4 Broadway Road
Evesham
Worcestershire WR11 6BH

A catalogue record for this book is available from the British Library.

ISBN 0 85305 344 8

Typeset in Monotype Bembo by
Pat Saunders, Little Gidding

Printed in Great Britain at the Guernsey Press, Guernsey, C.I.

PREFACE

As happy relationships are the key to the experience of joy in our lives, it seemed important to provide a simple book of principles that, when needed, could be there like an old friend. May this book serve you in good times, as well as when the road seems dark and threatening. There is an old Korean proverb that says, 'Even if the sky should fall, there is a way out.' There always is a way out if you are willing to see things differently. May this book bless you with a way out and the way in.

Warmest aloha,

CHUCK SPEZZANO
Hawaii, 1996

DAY 1

Those you dislike are on your team

The most important aspect of your life is your attitude, because your attitude is the direction in which you are heading. It is created out of continuous decisions made in a certain direction. Therefore, it is most important that you choose a life that has a giving, regenerating, youthening and abundant direction. If you do not, your chances of knowing love and happiness are slim.

Life can seem like a war in which you are fighting for your family, while others outside you threaten you and your security. But if you choose an attitude like that, it will subtly (or not so subtly) translate itself into your family and your relationship with your partner. You will not be safe from the competition, power struggle and fear that you see so blatantly existing outside your family. It is most important to choose an attitude that will unite you with your partner, your family and the outside world.

The spiritual insight of 'love your enemies' was brought to earth by Christ, but as a means psychologically to heal and transform situations it is little recognized, and even more rarely practised. You have the opportunity to turn your enemies into your allies, your team-mates and even your saviours. This is the highest attitude to take towards those around you. As you truly succeed with one person in your life by transforming them into your ally, you simultaneously evolve all of your other relationships into being more supportive and healthy.

Those you dislike represent a lesson you are being asked to learn. To learn this lesson advances your maturity, your confidence, your ability to make contact and your capacity to receive. To learn the lesson of turning a seeming enemy into an important ally advances your leadership, increases your power and truly helps world peace.

Exercise

Today, make the choice for those you dislike to be on your team. Begin to see them as vital parts of your happiness. If they lose, the team loses. If they lose, you will have to pay the bill. Life is a team sport. There is no area where the interconnection of relationships is not a determining factor. They must win and you must win for there to be ultimate happiness.

DAY 2

Trust turns everything to advantage

When a problem occurs it is because we have a split mind. The conscious mind wants to move forward but the subconscious mind is afraid of losing something to which we are attached. We then project out the subconscious part onto some person or situation which then seems to obstruct us. In truth, the obstruction is merely the objectification of our own ambivalence. This ambivalence shows itself as a lack of confidence.

Confidence turns problematic situations into merely 'something to handle'. It is trust that generates confidence. Trust is not being naive, which ignores information or intuition. Trust takes all of the situation in hand, no matter how seemingly negative, and begins to turn it to advantage. For trust, like faith, uses the power of your mind to begin to unfold the situation in a positive manner. Trust knows that no matter what the situation looks like, it is working for you. It is knowing this that allows you to see every advantage and benefit in the situation.

Trust is the opposite of control or power struggle. It does not attempt to change anyone to meet our needs or do it our way. If control has never been successful in the past, it is not likely to be successful now. Even in those times that we win and people do things our way, they lose their attractiveness and go into sacrifice. When they lose their attractiveness we also lose, and it begins to feel as if we are in sacrifice just being with them. When someone loses, typically they will bide their time until they can try to win and be on top again. Trust allows everyone to win. Trust is one of the primordial healing principles. There is no problem that trust could not heal.

Exercise

Today, turn the power of your mind towards someone you dislike and everything they do. When you begin to trust them and their actions, even the seeming malicious acts begin to work for you. Trust advances you and the situation.

Any time you think of that person, send trust. You do not have to know how the situation could possibly get better as that is not your job. Your job is to send your trust until you feel at peace. You may feel yourself going through many layers of feelings. If this occurs, it is very healing. If not, it makes it that much easier to heal.

DAY 3

See those you dislike in the present moment

The past is over. It doesn't exist except as you keep it alive. The past you keep alive is a past that serves a purpose for you. It is a past you are using in a certain way to justify your behaviour in the present.

Letting go of the past frees you from its negative effects. Most of us do not live at all in the present. If we did we would be happy. To live in the future is to live in fear. To live in the past is to feel guilty, bad and unworthy. At least ninety-eight per cent of the pain you feel is old pain you have dragged into the present. When it seems to come up in the present, it is really old pain that is triggered by something that is happening now.

The old patterns of pain are waiting to be unearthed and healed. To see someone in the present moment is to see them as if you were meeting them for the first time. It is to not hold the past against them. This allows you to see them in a new light, and it allows them to show how they have grown.

Most of us are living with the past dictating what the present is. The software of our bio-computer recapitulates the past into the present over and over again. This does not leave us much in the way of new possibilities or choices. Our present is held hostage by our past. Only by leaving the past behind do we have a chance of being happy. It is truly only the past we are healing. It is truly only our *perception* of the past that calls to be healed.

Exercise

Today, concentrate on seeing those you dislike in a new light, the present. Even if you spend time with someone you dislike today, let each moment go as it passes and see only the present. Grievances are only about the past, never about the present.

If you cannot let this grievance go, ask yourself if you have ever behaved like this. If you have, ask yourself what you must have been feeling to act in that fashion. Would you blame yourself for that behaviour knowing what feeling generated it?

DAY 4

You are using those you dislike to avoid the next step

In any power struggle, both sides are actually frightened to move forward, and so both sides fight to have things their way. They fight to gain control, 'knowing' their way is the best way. They are unwilling to consider how both sides are crucial for a new integration, a new answer. Even if the 'form' of the other's answer is absolutely wrong, the energy that their wrong answer holds with will be crucial for your success at the next step. Taking the next step rather than using those you dislike to avoid it, naturally integrates both sides into a successful new level.

We come into conflict with others when we try to get them to meet our needs, to do it our way. This creates competition which in turn creates a delay, because the other is looked at as the source of our happiness. Winning becomes everything. But in competition, when one person wins they then have to carry the one who loses. The focus is then on beating the other, rather than stepping forward where both could win equally.

The win–lose attitude creates delay. Only where there is win–win, is there not withdrawal, sabotage or a major attachment. Without win–win attitude, all of these dynamics are subconsciously at work. Power struggle disguises the attachment which blocks both intimacy and stepping forward. This attachment can be to a person, an old dream, way of life, or thing that we see somehow as a source of our happiness and as such we are afraid to let it go yet. But the attachment can never satisfy us. First of all, our need for the attachment makes it exceptionally hard to succeed and impossible to receive. And if we do get what we need we somehow feel disillusioned. It is not enough to satisfy us for long. Then we either seek a new attachment or feel like dying from the disappointment.

Exercise

Today, just ask yourself what attachment it is you are holding onto to be in this conflict, and see what pops into your head. If nothing pops in it is because it is so obvious you do not consider it, or it is too well defended to see. Spend some time dwelling on this theme to see what emerges.

DAY 5

Forgive to heal this problem

Many people are afraid to forgive because to them forgiving would mean they would remain a victim. They are afraid the other person would keep on doing what they were doing. Yet, forgiveness is what changes perception and experience; it would change the very pattern that got you into this problem. Forgiveness is not sacrifice, it is transformation and peace.

What you hold against those you dislike is judgement and grievance. Yet, only the guilty blame. The innocent see nothing to condemn. When we feel guilty, in an attempt to avoid suffering, we repress the feeling and project it out on someone else. Thus, what we hold against others is what we are judging in ourselves. Our grievances and projections on others give us access to finding areas of conflict inside ourselves that have somehow stopped us. We can work very hard in our lives without much reward to hide these buried subconscious elements which act as an invisible barrier that holds us back. Yet, all the hard work of compensations to hide our guilt is unrewarded. Only giving receives. Compensations to prove you are good, go unrewarded.

Our forgiveness of others releases our buried guilt. So,

rather than make someone you dislike be the scapegoat and lose the opportunity to heal hidden conflicts, today choose to do that which would free you both. If you continue to judge them, you will be stuck with what you have judged and remain in the same situation. Your guilt, although hidden, will continue to punish you.

Forgiveness protects your rights and your freedom while releasing your subconscious guilt. Forgiveness transforms the situation by transforming perception. Forgiveness reinstates everyone's innocence including your own.

Exercise

List three grievances that you have with another person. For each one ask yourself: 'Would I hold this against myself?' If the answer is no, you both are free.

Turn the forgiveness over to that part of your mind that has all the answers — your Higher Mind. Any time you think of someone you dislike just know the forgiveness is being handled for you. Enjoy the results.

DAY 6

Your anger is a form of control

Anger is a form of control. It is an attempt to get others to act in the way in which you want them to act, to meet your needs in the situation by doing it your way. This makes you feel secure and comfortable.

Anger makes the statement that we are perfectly justified in feeling and acting this way because another is to blame for our feelings. This form of immaturity blocks the ability to listen, learn, receive and change.

Our anger may show itself in different forms. It may show as direct attack, passive aggression, withdrawal, complaining or suffering. All of these forms are an attempt to gain control rather than a means to learn from the situation at hand and change. Even if your anger succeeded in controlling, it would only succeed in putting off a valuable lesson that wants to be learned. To put off a lesson allows it to become a trial later, but learning a lesson leads to greater confidence. Lack of confidence leads to control and anger in its many forms.

Your anger does not allow you to step forward because it has you trying to change the outside situation through control. This always takes longer and is not truly effective. As good a controller as you might be, you know you have not been that effective in controlling others over the years. Even if you have won the control game, when your partner lost, they also lost their attractiveness. By having an unattractive partner, you lost too.

Truly to change the world around you, you must change your mind. To do this at a subconscious level would mean that the person or situation would change without you having to control or dominate.

Exercise

Today, be willing to recognize that your anger just does not work. Take a step in maturity, a step towards seeing that anger is never justified, and pardon always is.

See yourself as making the choice to step forward where both your needs and other people's needs can be met in a whole new way. See yourself as stepping forward to a new level of success. Feel the confidence that comes with stepping forward to a new level. None of us knows what this step looks like until we step forward, but when we step forward things are always better.

DAY 7

Your anger hides deeper feelings

Anger is a defensive feeling that is meant to protect deeper feelings such as hurt, guilt, deadness, fear and frustration. If you allow yourself to know what the deeper feeling is and experience it, the anger, that either attacks or withdraws, falls away. If we become interested in knowing ourselves, we can chose an attitude of being willing to experience our more primordial emotions and resolve them.

It is a step in integrity to wish to know the emotions buried within us. We have been carrying them for many years, expending energy on them and not always keeping them under control. They always lead us into situations where they get triggered so they can be resolved. We then have an important choice to make: either we use the situation as an opportunity to learn and heal, thus being open to much greater learning and success; or we use our feelings as justification for attacking another. Only those who blame themselves accuse or attack others. The healed and innocent have no need to obstruct their learning and growth in this fashion.

As you begin to discover the emotions inside you, you begin to discover your self-defeating patterns. As you discover your self-defeating patterns, you find your self-concepts. Self-concepts are either positive or negative.

Positive self-concepts are compensations for how negative we feel about ourselves. They try to prove we are really good people. But to the extent we are caught up in proving our goodness, our negative self-concepts are implied; what you try to prove you do not fully believe.

Exercise

Be aware of any forms of anger today: aggression, withdrawal, passive aggression, suffering and any form of victimization. Be willing to experience whatever buried feelings there are underneath the anger. Ask yourself how old those feelings are and how old you were when these feelings began. Ask yourself about the pattern or compensation that has existed around these emotions. Ask yourself what self-concepts you have about yourself (positive or negative) that these emotions have supported. Make new decisions about these self-concepts using truth as your guide.

DAY 8

Your grievances hide unfinished business from within the family

Any unfinished business that was within your family as you grew up will be brought into your present relationships. It has long been known in therapeutic circles that bosses and authority figures 'take the heat' for unfinished business with fathers and mothers. At this point in your life, you may consciously feel quite different about the parent with whom you had the original problem. But if there is buried judgement, pain or guilt, it will tend to show up again in whatever situation you are in now in which there is a chance of getting the old pain out and transmitted.

If you realize that there is a pattern involved, it will serve to lessen the attack you make on others. Then you can bring your attention back to the only place where the problem can really be healed, which is inside yourself. If you take responsibility for this conflict in your life, your responsibility can change the situation.

Even if nothing readily comes to mind about a conflict from your original family (that which is subconscious does not always readily lend itself to consciousness), be willing to examine your life and your pattern of relationships. Do your present feelings remind you of feelings that have arisen in your life in the past?

The present situation is an excellent opportunity to heal the pattern, to not compound any existing patterns and certainly to not begin any new problem patterns that will later have to be cleared up. This situation serves as an excellent opportunity for healing, lessening your inner conflict and stress, and graduating you to a new level of consciousness.

Exercise

Imagine that someone you dislike is standing in front of you. Imagine now that what you see is actually only a dislikeable costume and that if you pulled off the mask, the person with whom you had the original conflict would appear. Now as you are ready, reach over to the person and pull off the mask . . . Who is there? Ask this person: 'How may I help you?'

Endeavour to accomplish the essence of this request for the person, first in your imagination and then in life, especially as it serves both of your interests. If, in the rare case that their request seems destructive, keep asking them the purpose of their request until you get to the very essence which will serve you both.

DAY 9

Someone you dislike is your projection

This lesson is of special interest to those who have a deep interest in growth, change and transformation. The principle is really a willingness to see everyone and everything that happens as a learning situation. It requires a willingness to see everyone and every situation as a projection of your subconscious mind and, at times, your unconscious mind. As this makes the outer world a reflection of the inner mind, the outer world can be changed by changing your mind within.

If you remember that each person you see outside yourself actually represents a part of your mind that has been judged, fragmented, dis-identified, buried and projected outward, then you can be much more ready and willing to do the work to win these pieces of yourself back. This occurs through integrating the missing or repressed parts.

Many people are frightened of integrating parts of themselves that they are projecting onto others because they are afraid of bringing in what seems so negative. It is the act of integration that transforms any negativity into that which provides an inoculation or vaccination against further negativity of this sort. Through this integration you learn the lesson that is being provided, and then progress on to the next lesson, the next projection, the next step, the next challenge.

This is begun by seeing no one's interest as separate from your own. This is furthered through such forms of healing as understanding, acceptance, giving, forgiving, letting go, trust, communication, integration, commitment, truth, receiving, grace and responsiveness. It is hindered through fear, guilt, suffering, pain, selfishness, evil, authority conflict, control, hurt, grievance/need and all of the things that seem to generate and be generated by separativeness.

Exercise

Imagine that an someone you dislike is standing before you, but instead of seeing their body or personality, you see the trillions of light particles that make up their being. Experience this glowing sentient light as their essence.

Now see yourself in the same way.

Next imagine these two lights were joining together. As they completely join, see yourself emerging in a whole new way with a great deal more confidence. See and feel yourself as having integrated and thus dispersed the negative qualities, while accentuating and multiplying the many positive ones that come with integration.

DAY 10

Your grievances hide your guilt

This is an important lesson, for it is guilt that keeps us in sacrifice. It is guilt that creates all forms of suffering. This is the guilt that comes from any unfinished business of the past, anything about which we feel bad. This is the guilt that arises out of separation and self-deception. This is the guilt that causes conflict because only the self-deceived could be in conflict. We live in a world of conflict, self-deception and illusion as to what has true worth.

Since guilt is such an uncomfortable feeling, we typically deny it, hide it and project it out on others. We can only accuse someone of doing that which we think we have been doing. We can only judge those on whom we project our own unfinished and hidden conflicts. That is why recognizing our innocence is so important both for ourselves and others. Innocence could free us of pain, scarcity and the separation that generates conflicts. It could literally save the world.

We can use our grievances and conflicts as a way to discover where our hidden conflicts and guilt are. Resolving these inner conflicts and guilt is a very easy way to resolve outer problems and conflicts. Properly used, our grievances can be a way to find guilt that is so well buried we would have no other way of finding it. Your grievances can assist you to heal yourself in spite of denial, because your grievances point to your guilt.

Exercise

Think of a particular grievance you have. Spend time now 'owning' that particular behaviour pattern as if it were yours, albeit subconsciously. Notice how you treat yourself as if you were doing it all the time. Feel the feeling that this generates until there is no longer an emotional charge on it. Do this until you can say: 'Yes, this is me. I'm just like this.' Now dwell on this behaviour until you can begin to feel innocent about this behaviour.

DAY 11

A power struggle is a place where everyone eventually loses

Power struggles, especially those in relationships, have no winners. If you win, the other person goes into the losing position. From the losing position they also lose what attractiveness they have, and they typically enter in a sacrifice position. Either way, when someone around you loses, you end up paying the bill, or it is only a matter of time before they seek to ambush you and regain domination.

In a power struggle at least one of the parties feels badly. Because they feel badly, they look around for someone to blame.

No one wants to feel pain, and it takes a great deal of maturity not to react when you are in pain or when someone has struck out at you. But it is possible, and it allows you to transform and unfold situations in positive ways. It is a sign of maturity. Even while you are in pain and tempted to react and strike out, you can ask yourself: 'What would help the situation?' If you listen you will notice that a way is being intuitively suggested to you. If you respond according to the quiet voice within, you will find the situation unfolding positively. If you choose to move forward rather than strike back, your healing and your life can take a step forward.

Today, turn any power struggle away from its ability to stop your forward movement, into a situation of growth. If you are in a power struggle, listen to the voice from your Higher Mind. If you are experiencing any kind of problem today, listen to your Higher Mind. Take five minutes today to ask and listen for the solution. The solution is always being offered if you have the willingness to listen. Of course, one of the greatest arts is to be able to do this listening in the midst of your pain.

Once you see the possibility of having everyone in the situation win, it will occur and you will be inspired by the results. Being willing to change will add to your ability to receive, succeed and love.

DAY 12

Those you dislike are not holding you back

Those you dislike are not holding you back, you are. As a matter of fact, the extent to which you think they are holding you back is the extent to which you are using them to hold yourself back. The only conspiracy against you is a self-conspiracy.

It takes a great deal of maturity to realize that everything happens for the best, all things considered. Many of us go through major lessons, challenges, trials and tests. A trial is just an unlearned lesson that is now coming around finally to be learned. A test is a major opportunity. It could actually be a life or death situation or a situation where we would feel crushed if we do not pass the test. To pass the test is similar to passing an initiation in that we springboard forward in consciousness. Your difficult relationships are providing such opportunities.

If life is about the expansion of consciousness so that we might grow in love and joy, then this is just an opportunity to transform yourself and move to a whole new level. If you think those you dislike are holding you back, then you have some other idea of what life and happiness is all about. You hold other values, attitudes or hidden agendas to gain love, joy and happiness. Actually, we work hard for so many things that in the end do not even satisfy us, much less give us love, happiness and joy. What gives us joy is love, creativity, giving, receiving, forgiveness and our purpose. In giving and receiving there is a natural flow forward. Forgiveness ends fear and conflict, and creates the vital change needed for movement forward towards joy and happiness.

Not to choose transformation in the face of your problem is to dig in your heels and to try to get the rest of the world to change for you. It did not work for us as children and it will not work for us as adults. Adult tantrums that take the form of anger and aggression, or feeling hurt and attacked, are no more successful than our childhood tantrums.

Exercise

Now is the time to make a choice to take that significant step forward. Now is the time to be willing to leap forward to a new level. Now is the time that forgiveness will change your perception and increase your learning.

DAY 13

Those you dislike have come to help

Those you dislike are here to help, and only your attitude or perspective would signal otherwise. Let us start by saying that your general purpose in life is similar to everyone's: love, happiness, abundance, joy and evolution. Then comes the question of how one achieves that.

Let us say that someone you dislike is over-sensitive, cantankerous and aggressive. Your thought is: 'If I want to be happy I must stay away from this person, because every time I am around them, they say or do something that upsets me, and I am not happy any more.' This attitude, which may ultimately be true, will not further your happiness or your maturity if you do not first apply some basic principles to help the situation evolve. First of all, you are not placed in a situation in which there is no answer. As impossible as some situations seem, there is always an answer where everyone can win. Secondly, you are not where you are by accident, but by design. You are in this situation because there is some vital lesson in it for you to learn. You might as well learn it now.

This situation points to a long-standing conflict within yourself. Without someone to project this conflict onto, it may have taken many more years for you to get in touch with why you just are not happy. If that person were gone you would still have the conflict inside that defies your best efforts at happiness, and you would not know why. Your pain is the beginning of the healing process. It lets you know of a place where you need healing, a place where you are not harmless. Do not lose this opportunity, only to have to face it later.

All conflicts stem from old broken hearts. All conflicts stem from unmet needs, and your needs are expressions of fear, demand and attack. Your needs are not only met, but transcended, through your forgiveness, your giving forth of the very thing you think you need.

Exercise

In this situation that you are presently in, ask yourself intuitively: 'How old was I when this conflict began?' Ask yourself: 'Who was present with me when this occurred?' Ask yourself: 'What was it that occurred when this conflict began?' Examine the needs that everyone in the situation was feeling. What did you then decide about yourself, life, relationships, etc.? What you decided became your beliefs, and the world has recapitulated itself in terms of those beliefs. What you believe, you perceive. How you perceive comes form these beliefs and you act accordingly. This brings a response according to your belief and your belief is thus compounded and reinforced. Make new choices about what you want to believe.

DAY 14

Sacrifice is a form of counterfeit bonding

Sacrifice can be the letting go of a lower form for something greater or more spiritual. When seen in its true light, this is not a loss. The sacrifice referred to in this book is an untrue form, a psychological mistake, an attempt to make others lose or sacrifice even more than you.

Sacrifice is giving without receiving. Psychologically, to give is to receive and to receive is to give. It is really give/receive. Giving allows us to connect or realize the connections we have with those around us. Bonding is not something you do, it is something that is. It is a natural part of who you are with others. That is unless there is a conflict within that separates you from these others.

Psychodynamically, at the heart of any problem you find fear/separation. To heal either the fear or the separation is to transform the problem. Sacrifice is a mistaken solution for the need for inclusion. It gives fusion, a collusional confusion of personality boundaries. Fusion is counterfeit union or love. It comes from a position of sacrifice, built on guilt and trauma where we lost the realization of bonding and began to sacrifice in an attempt to regain intimacy. Fusion is a counterfeit closeness that secretly thirsts for revenge.

If you are in sacrifice with another person in any form, you have a solution that will not last. Do not compromise, as you will both feel as if you have lost. Come to resolution. Come to a solution that is balanced, where you both win. Sacrifice seeks closeness, but breeds resentment. Sacrifice is based on your guilt and only the innocence of everyone involved will allow for a solution and a true bonding. Do not settle for less. Do not give up or adjust to the situation. Want and choose the bonding. Choose everyone's innocence. Do not settle for sacrifice.

Exercise

Ask your Higher Mind to carry you back to your centre. Ask your Higher Mind to carry those you dislike back to their centres. Ask your Higher Mind to carry everyone from the original event back to their centres.

Feel the peace that comes to you as you reach your centre. What could take you months to attain would only take seconds for your Higher Mind. Imagine you could see or feel the Light or Spirit inside you. Then you feel everyone in their centres, past and present. Imagine the Light inside you is sending out tendrils of light and connecting with all the others in the event. Take some time just to enjoy this feeling.

DAY 15

Those you dislike are not stopping you from receiving love

Those you dislike are not stopping you from receiving love. You are. They are not stealing your spouse's love from you. You only get the love you allow yourself to receive. If someone seems to be intercepting the love coming to you, that is only how it seems on a conscious level. In truth we always receive love if we feel worthy of it and are not afraid of it. We use others to people our conspiracy against ourselves.

Where someone else seems to have unnaturally heavy claims on your spouse, there is a case of fusion going on. This is a blurring of the natural boundaries between two people. It is a form of sacrifice and hidden, or not so hidden, resentment. This speaks of an imbalance in their family when they were growing up. But this could only be happening because there was also such an imbalance in your family.

Fusion is the root of co-dependency problems where one person is the enabler and the other is the identified problem person or addictive personality. Fusion is a place of counterfeit intimacy that does not allow receiving and generates an overburdening sense of loyalty that we mistake for love. This mistake keeps us chained to people or situations and actually creates an 'enabling' situation rather than a helpful one. The enabling situation is where you are ostensibly the helper, but are secretly reinforcing the problem to keep yourself needed. You do not actually want the other person to change, get better and move forward because their movement would force you to do the same or be left behind. Your fear of moving forward is just as strong as that of the identified problem person.

Exercise

Close your eyes and feel or imagine being back with your original family in the situation you have unearthed. Ask your Higher Mind to bring you back to your centre in this situation. Ask that your Higher Mind bring your whole family back to its centre in this situation.

Now ask that in your present situation you be brought back to your centre, and that everyone in this situation be carried back to their centre. You will know when this is complete because you will feel peace, even when thinking of those you dislike.

DAY 16

Joining with those you dislike will create healing

The only real problem we suffer from is separation – seeing our interests as different from others. Dynamically, this separation, which is synonymous with fear and attack thoughts, generates the proliferation of problems that we experience. When we feel separate, we act in a competitive way to further our interests, disregarding and objectifying those around us. Even winning the competition and having more than others, naturally leads to alienation. The sense of separation becomes more pronounced by either winning or losing. Only co-operation and mutuality lead to joining and intimacy.

Joining knows that any fusion or any competition is actually a way to avoid taking the next step. Both are ways you seek to take from another. This delays you and has you looking in the wrong direction for your happiness. You then fall into the biggest mistake of assigning to others a secondary place in the 'movie' of your life, and thereby making them merely objects to meet your needs. This will lead to upset if they do not accept the script you assigned to them, or boredom and the eventual sacrifice of having to 'carry' them if they do.

Joining, on the other hand, really moves you forward. By joining with another, you are both brought to a new level of intimacy and a new level of confidence. There is a commonweal that springs up in intimacy that gives one a feel of common goal, a common humanity and shared family. It is the beginning of the experience that all of us are here for each other. When things are at their highest and best we seem to know that. Joining gives you the feeling of winning together that is both love and the joy that comes from connectedness.

Exercise

Imagine someone you dislike was across a large room from you and that the distance between you was in reality the distance, separateness and judgement between you. Imagine each step towards that person is a step in healing that distance. Take step after step towards them in your mind's eye as you feel willing to bridge the gap between you. If you feel resistance, just feel the discomfort on until it is gone and ask your Higher Mind for help. As you finally reach that person, look in their eyes and see the child inside them that wants your love, that implores your love, that invites your love. Reach out and take their hands. Hear their call for help, their call to be saved, their call to save you. Imagine now that who is before you is a part of yourself that you judged, fragmented and repressed, and that you have finally come to redeem yourself, to forgive yourself. Integrate the part of you that was lost that has been causing an invisible barrier in your forward movement.

DAY 17

Life is about happiness and healing

Life is about happiness and joy. But happiness is as elusive as a butterfly. To chase it is to scare it away. To sit quietly or follow your true purpose is to allow it to come to you naturally. Happiness comes out of love and creativity. It comes out of the fulfilment of living your personal purpose and being part of the world's evolution. When you are not in happiness you can use the lack of it as an indicator of when you are called upon to heal, learn and change. Healing, learning and changing bring about the conditions needed for happiness.

Let us take your bad relationships again. If you are not happy in this situation as yet, you are probably caught in a chronic painful pattern. Now the next major dynamic to examine is actually the fear of moving forward which this hidden or not so hidden guilt supports. Forgiveness of self and others naturally moves you forward. Guilt and blame support your being stuck. One purpose of guilt and blame is that you do not have to move forward and face that which frightens you.

To have a fear of the future is another way to place undue emphasis on yourself. Undue emphasis will support a glamour which takes the form either of exaggerated personality or disappointment/shame. Any area in which you are not succeeding, is an area in which you are actually succeeding in getting some subconscious agendas met, which are more important to you than your success. These other agendas are to make up for the past and are hidden forms of *getting* rather than receiving or succeeding.

Each step forward that you take allows a little more of your personality to disappear and your love and creativity to appear. This is really the love and creativity of heaven shining through you, gracing you and those around you. When it is you personally doing something, it is your personality doing it, which means you never get truly to receive but only to indulge. Indulgence is only half of a vicious indulgence–sacrifice circle. Feeding one demands a feeding for the other.

Exercise

Today, examine the situation again. What is being called for? Forgiveness? Centering? Taking the next step? Letting go?

Whatever it is, it is not something for you to do. Do not trade in one problem for another. Let your Higher Mind do it for you, through you. Do not hold yourself back by exaggerating yourself positively or negatively. If you are not in your own way, happiness comes to you.

DAY 18

Those you dislike are not traps

Those you dislike are not traps unless you make them into traps. A trap is a situation in which you are stuck that keeps you obsessing about it rather than moving forward. It is an obstruction to peace, and it is peace from which joy, love and movement forward are generated.

A trap can be used to stop you from moving forward because you are frightened of the next step. A trap can be used to block a gift, opportunity or talent because you are afraid of the level of surrender these benefits call for in you. A trap is built on guilt, some kind of bad feeling that keeps you withdrawn and out of the flow of life. A trap keeps you self-conscious when others most need your help. It keeps you self-centred and even selfishly indulgent when it is most important that you extend yourself both for yourself and others.

One of the basic ways to move out of a trap is first to realize that you have got yourself into one. A trap is a problem for which you are afraid to get the solution because it is asking you to change in some way. Whenever a problem emerges a solution emerges at the same time. If you have the courage to accept it everything prospers. To find the solution immediately is to not abuse time. If you waste time, time wastes you. Once you realize you are in a trap you can use your most powerful tool, the power of choice. You can choose not to be trapped.

Exercise

In any situation in your life where there is a trap, use these statements to move out of your obsession and into peace. Use these words of power to help move you forward. They will remove the trap, or at least a major layer of it. Use them as many times as is necessary. Fill the words with your energy, your will and the power of your choice.

'I will not use this as a trap. I will not use this to hold me back. But I will use it as a means to truth, peace and leaping forward.'

DAY 19

Competition is a form of delay

This is a most important concept as it is interconnected with the basis of all pain, attachment. Competition is not only present in every form of separation (which generates fear), it is also present in every attachment, every idol that we see as a source of our happiness.

Competition actually hides fear of the next step. When it is present the consuming desire becomes to beat your opponent by winning, and so the real issue is not faced. Instead of facing forward and finding the integration or partnership where everyone can win, there is a facing towards the one with whom you are competing or are in conflict, thinking that 'besting' them will somehow give you what you need.

Competition begins in an unbonded family. The fear, scarcity and separation dictate certain family roles that are both personal compensations and an attempt to balance the family. But these defences have no success and at best can only maintain the present family dilemma. At the bottom of everything lies the fear of loss that begets scarcity and competition.

In competition we are seeking to meet our needs through the other, and the other is seeking to meet their needs through us. Yet this obscures the fact that if one of us were to just take the next step, both would be moved forward to a new plateau, a new integration and understanding where both could win together. There is no relationship that is in trouble that does not have some form of competition. Competition insidiously destroys relationships.

Competition is always quick to find fault and correct another. Correction is a form of arrogance that keeps us looking for mistakes in those around us rather than looking forward to see where our next step is. Whenever we are correcting another it is a sure sign we are avoiding what needs correction in us. The best competition is not a competition at all but a desire to excel and expand personal or global horizons. It looks on opponents as fellow players that help to call out the very best in you.

Exercise

Examine areas of competition in your life. Write down self-concepts you are trying to prove about your self. What self-concepts do these hide? When you discover major negative self-concepts, remember that these too are merely concepts you are trying to prove to hide your true goodness and power. We hide our true goodness and power because we are afraid to be that good or to have it all out of fear of what might be expected of us. Discover and experience these truths about yourself.

DAY 20

*Understanding opens the door to forgiveness
and appreciation opens the door to love*

You have probably noticed by your aggression, attack
thoughts and victimization (which is but another form
of attack) that you are not completely harmless. You
may have noticed that even your sacrifice in this
situation is actually a manipulation to get the other to
lose the game and have to sacrifice more than you so
you can get your way. Those who are whole make no
demands.

You are not here in this situation by accident, but by
design. You can do much to further yourself and others
by your willingness to understand all the levels of what
is taking place. Once someone understands, they feel no
need to forgive, realizing that there has just been a
mistake. Life is telling you through these circumstances
about an aspect within you that can be straightened out.
If you refuse the lesson, it will typically become a trial
for you. Here is a chance to learn of your wholeness,
which this conflict is obscuring from you.

Giving your appreciation is another possible way of
moving through a conflict (or one layer of the conflict
at a time). This occurs because appreciation sets up a
flow, whereas judgement and grievance lock you into

the situation. The appreciation may only be at the level of discovering that you have finally identified this conflict inside you that has been eating away at you without your awareness, and stealing energy to keep the conflict locked away.

Exercise

Imagine that you are someone you dislike. Imagine what it is like waking up in the morning as them . . . how things feel, what the world looks like to them, how their day goes, what they are thinking about, where they feel threatened. Imagine all of their interactions and feelings until they go to bed at night. Take at least ten minutes for this exercise.

List in your mind or on paper all of the things you really appreciate about that person. Any good qualities they have, any kindnesses they may have done for you or your family, or any support they may have given are likely areas to explore. Dwell on these things, or on just one of these things if it especially stands out for you. This appreciation will move you forward.

DAY 21

Your balance helps more than just yourself

Balance is a state of mind where peace resides. It is unruffled by the ups and downs that fortune brings. It is neither passive nor static, but responsive and connected. It gives and receives. While not relying on itself, it has both the courage to lead and the intelligence to allow group strength and Higher Mind to achieve success rather than only cope with the status quo.

Your balance and evenness are a benefit to your partner and family, as they can rely on this steadiness rather than the vagaries of emotion and mood. When reactive or aggressive energy comes your way, balance calmly recognizes attack as a call for help, a chance to grow and strengthen, and an opportunity for new learning and greater contact.

Emotions have a way of triggering each other. This is obvious in cases of fear or anger. A person who is willing not to buy into a reactive emotional situation is the person who can change or begin to change the pattern. This person, by their balance and vision, can close the door to hysteria and the attack of reactive emotion.

Every family has a group-mind which is constantly

seeking to balance itself through the actions of its members. One person striving for truth and a responsive balance, rather than always feeding the family drama, can do much to unfold a family towards its purpose.

The whole world is inextricably interconnected. An act of kindness, generosity or love adds to the light of the whole world. What you do with those around you with whom you are interconnected can bless the entire world.

Exercise

Imagine the family you grew up with, standing around you in a circle. Know that they are reflections of your own mind. As aspects of your mind have them come to you one by one, joining you and melting into you.

Next imagine any people you are having problems with and then once again have each of them stand in a circle, come up to you, melt into you and integrate with you.

DAY 22

An attack on someone you dislike is really an attack on your partner

Any attack on another is actually an attack meant for your partner or the one closest to you. It is much easier to displace upset onto someone seemingly outside your relationship, than to be aware and deal with the aspect that is incomplete and troubling you in your relationship. Looking at your grievance with another in this way is a way of making that which is subconscious conscious so that you can deal with it.

Also, what you hold against anyone, you are actually holding against everyone, which includes your partner. If your mate was doing what you are upset at others for doing, you would be holding it against your mate also. And you actually are, because the distance you keep from one person actually keeps a wedge between you and everyone.

To forgive something in anyone is to forgive it in everyone, including yourself. To forgive an issue is to transform your perception of it so that you either no longer perceive it as a problem or you perceive it as a call for help to which you can easily respond. Either way, it leads to peace.

It takes a natural intuitiveness, or a good level of communication, to ferret out the hidden issue between you and your partner, but it is truly worth doing. This is because the hidden issue is affecting you even though you are not aware of it. Awareness of a problem is half the battle. It is also important to be aware of the fact that as soon as a problem appears, so does the answer. While our actual experience may differ from this, it is important to know that the principle is true and our answers will appear as we are truly ready to accept them. The amount of time it takes for us to get an answer is the amount of time it takes for us to have confidence about the next step, the next level of success.

Exercise

Conjure up the negative feelings you have towards someone you dislike. Examine whether you have experienced the feelings that you are now experiencing before. With whom did you experience these feelings and in what regard? Does this mean that a pattern of such feelings has existed at least since childhood? As you become aware of this pattern ask your Higher Mind to clear it for you. When you take full responsibility for an experience in your life, you can then ask your Higher Mind to clear it for you.

DAY 23

On both sides of a conflict people are acting in opposite ways and feeling the same thing

In any conflict people may be acting in completely opposite fashions, such as victimizer–victim, fight–flight or hysterical–stoical. Yet both parties are feeling the exact same emotion, even if they are not consciously aware of it. For instance, there is as much anger or violence in a victim as there is in a victimizer, and fear generates both fight and flight. In any conflict we feel as if our position is correct and we fight for being right. Yet, if we recognized that we were actually feeling the same thing that our opponent is feeling, it can become a point of sharing, mutual identification and even the beginning of agreement.

The first step is to recognize what it is that you are feeling, remembering that such feelings as anger actually hide deeper emotions such as hurt, fear or guilt. One of you may be acting in a dissociated manner so as not to feel the pain, but your defensiveness belies the pain. As you get in touch with the feelings you are feeling, you have the basis for understanding what the other person is feeling, and thus why they are acting as they are. You also have the basis for communication because you have a point of mutuality.

The second step is to invite them into communication where this is possible. For example: 'Are you feeling afraid?' or 'I have been feeling guilty for some reason, and it has interfered with our relationship. Have you been feeling negative feelings too?' Many times it is more successful if you share your feelings and check to see if they are feeling similarly.

This is a first point of joining, and a place where your understanding can begin to give you confidence. It can also be the beginning of uncovering the self-deception that is present on both sides in any conflict.

Exercise

Get in touch with what it is you are feeling and experiencing in this conflict. Begin communication around this experience, looking for a place of mutuality. When this is found, both of you will not look at the other as the enemy. Communication is the beginning of forgiveness. You can even realize partnership by moving through this experience together in communication.

DAY 24

Communication – the heart of healing

Because communication leads to forgiveness, it is the heart of healing. About eighty-five per cent of all conflict seems to be healed by clarification of what you are experiencing and your intentions and goals in the situation. The other fifteen per cent represents areas of chronic conflict for both parties that have now surfaced to be healed. Fighting for your way, overtly or covertly, does not lead to either maturity or progress. While it is important not to let oneself be overrun, fighting suggests a weakened, fearful and immature position.

Communication is at the heart of a position where both parties can win in a mature and more integrated fashion. The first aspect of communication is the willingness to set a goal in which both parties can win, and not stop before that empowering goal is reached by both. If there is a sense of sacrifice or compromise (which indicates the communication has not come to resolution) there will be a feeling, sooner or later, that one or both of you has lost, and the conflict will resume.

The next step in communication is to communicate what is not working or what it is you are upset about. Recognizing you are never upset for the reason you think allows you to reassure your partner in this communication. The purpose of your communication is not to trigger their guilt, but to come to resolution. If you then 'own' what is not working by taking responsibility for your experience, you inspire your partner with a willingness to continue communication now and in the future. They understand that the purpose of the communication is not to make them wrong.

To have a successful relationship you must have successful communication. It is an essential factor in maturity and evolution. So, you might as well decide to become an expert in communication for it will benefit your love life, your career and your family.

Exercise

Decide to become an expert on communication. It will serve you your whole life. Practice the principles of communication in this lesson with those around you. You may want to write them down so they are available to you.

Practice these principles especially with someone you dislike. Let them know you value the relationship enough to communicate to make it better. Appreciate their willingness to work with you on this. If they are totally uncooperative, you can ask someone close to you to role-play them. Have them just 'tune in' to the person you dislike, paying special attention to that person's emotional experience as they communicate.

DAY 25

Expectations are hidden demands

Whenever you find yourself frustrated or disappointed, it is because you have an expectation of someone or something. It is a judgement that something should be different than it is. This type of response is an expectation, and it creates stress. An expectation is some form of 'should', 'have to', 'need to', 'ought to' or 'must'. It is a demand on yourself or others.

When demand is put upon someone to do something under duress (a form of sacrifice which does not allow them to receive), most people will acquiesce. Or they will not do what is demanded of them because they feel pressured. This includes when we make demands on ourselves.

To ask, invite or inspire others opens up the flow of life, rather than trying to push or force it. Expectations block communications because they are a form of force which demands that others change to meet your needs. This creates resistance and power struggle and stops forward progress.

Demands come out of our needs; wholeness would make no demands. We demand of others that which we are not doing ourselves. For instance, if we expect someone to love us, it is because we are not loving ourselves. When we demand rather than choose or prefer, we push people away from us. Demanding our needs to be met by others demonstrates a conflict within us. Even if we get that which we have demanded, it would not satisfy or empower us. Only that which we give/receive can do that.

An expectation is hidden pain that will surface sooner or later, bringing its burden with it. This is why letting go of attachments allows us to move forward easily. Letting go is merely the recognition that an illusion cannot make us happy. To let go is not to throw away, but merely to place things in their proper perspective and in their right relationship. Anything else is an illusion, and when we spend a great deal of time and energy investing in an illusion, we are sure to be disillusioned.

Exercise

Examine the 'shoulds' and 'need tos' that you have in relation to others. Now start 'burning' away these attitudes, turning them over to your Higher Mind.

DAY 26

Guilt is merely a trap

As human beings we feel guilty about a myriad of things. Virtually all the bad feelings we have, such as sadness, hurt, sacrifice, needs and fear, also carry an adjunctive feeling of guilt. Guilt keeps us living in the past rather than the present moment. Guilt does not see mistakes that need correction; it sees badness that deserves and needs punishment.

Guilt is such a painful feeling that we typically project it out and see others as worthy of punishment. Guilt easily hides under judgements and grievances.

Bottom line, guilt hides fear because where we are guilty, we are actually afraid to face the next step. All of us have loads of guilt, but guilt is untrue and it keeps us from repenting, learning the lesson and correcting the mistake. Guilt invests itself in separateness as the guilty are ever alone in their guilt.

With someone you dislike there is guilt or bad feeling, and you have been using this as a trap. Refuse to allow this to continue. Do not use it on yourself or the other person, or allow them to use it on you. Guilt will hide the truth in the situation. The truth will allow you to respond in such a way as to move things forward. Be willing to get back on the path of life and take the next step. Let no vestige of guilt which hides in grievance or judgement hinder your unfoldment. Let no areas where you are working hard, but making no progress, hide guilt and hamper you. Let none of the overcompensations of sacrifice and untrue giving hide guilt. Let no demand or attack camouflage it.

Exercise

Today, focus on areas of guilt, sacrifice and grievances, especially in regard to situations with those you dislike. If you find any areas about which you feel bad, then choose no longer to use this as a trap, but move forward to give/receive in life again. Be willing to learn any lessons or correct any mistakes as you do so. You can do this through the power of choice.

Be willing to release your grievances and the guilt hiding underneath them in order to move forward. Choose to let these grievances go to improve your life and your relationships. As you let grievances towards others go it removes the subconscious guilt that both keeps you feeling bad and generates painful experiences to pay off guilt.

DAY 27

Acceptance heals conflicts

Wherever there is a conflict there is something that you will not accept. Your rejection or resistance actually creates the feeling of hurt or rejection and, of course, 'what you resist persists'. Your resistance keeps the conflict from changing or unfolding. You are locked into the very thing you can't stand until, paradoxically, you accept it. When you stop trying to change someone and either accept them as they are or actually do what is true for you, the person or situation changes.

Conflict is a fight for who is to be dominant and who is to be in sacrifice. Even being in sacrifice yourself is an attempt to get the other person then to sacrifice more than you.

As you accept, you allow the situation to progress, unfold and evolve to the next step. Yet many are afraid that if they accept the situation, it will continue unabated. But, it is only your resistance and sacrifice that allow a painful situation to continue. Sacrifice is a form of losing in a conflict in order either to be the morally superior person or to lose now so that the other might lose bigger in the long run. On the other hand, acceptance allows the outer situation to unfold as you integrate the inner fragmented part of your mind that helped create the conflict on the outside.

Exercise

Think of someone you dislike, and look for that to which you are attached and haven't been willing to let go. Look for what it is you refuse to accept and would rather fight about. Acknowledge what it is you could lose by not accepting this (e.g., being beyond this situation, having the wisdom and power of successfully graduating from this situation, losing contact with your Higher Mind and its ability to find a solution where you both win in seemingly impossible situations, release from fear in situations like this, etc.)

Make another choice about what you want now.

DAY 28

Your purpose awaits you

Our conflict distracts us from our personal purpose and evolution. Personal service and world evolution become ancillary to us during the drama of a conflict. Many times we create the conflict because we are afraid of our personal purpose and so seek to distract ourselves away from it.

Our purpose is never more than we can handle, though the thought of it is sometimes both thrilling and frightening. Our purpose is not specifically things we do, though that may be a part of it. It is something we are; an aspect of our beingness that radiates out to the world. Fear of purpose is the underlying cause of the vast majority of conflicts, problems, traps and distractions. Because we are afraid that we are not 'big' enough or confident enough to make a difference or to accomplish our purpose, we create traumatic or problematic situations that keep us from taking the next step, giving ourselves to what is truly important and living our purpose.

Our purpose is about happiness. If we are not happy, our purpose begins with forgiveness, harmlessness, healing and service, so that happiness can be achieved. In addition to happiness, our personal purpose has to do with that focus or function which only we can fulfil. All of these aspects lead to happiness and fulfilment. To change our conflicts into something that adds to personal and world purpose, it would require dedicating ourselves to harmlessness and healing the problem.

Living our purpose allows for a visionary state of being. This is a level of love and creativity that provides a positive future, an expanded awareness and an excitement about life and other people.

Most people shy away from any thought of their purpose for fear that they will have to do it, or fear of losing something to which they are attached. But vision is not something you do, it is something that is done through you. In vision there is a sense of life living you, rather than you living life. It feels like you are your best self.

Exercise

Most of the problems and traumas of your life have been there to hide your life purpose, yet the resolution of these problems and patterns helps unveil and fulfil your life's purpose. Choose no longer to let this most precious gift and means of fulfilment be hidden from you. Choose to know yourself and your gift to life. Choose to know how you fit into the unfolding world plan and purpose.

DAY 29

Those you dislike have come to save you

We shall take a look at a more advanced concept today. It approaches your conflict from a new perspective. As you change your perspective, your perception changes, and thus the situation itself. At some level, all healing is a change in the way we see things.

To change your perspective, it will be necessary that you be willing to give up being right. You cannot be right and have a healing too. Your change of perspective is the basis of your successful resolution of this situation. This takes the readiness to be a willing learner – even a happy learner!

Today's new perspective comes from seeing those you dislike as coming to save you. They are coming to save you, in that they are giving you an opportunity to clear out a conflict within you that has been eating away at you, using up inner resources, and stopping your forward progress with an invisible wall that has thwarted your best efforts to move beyond it. Now the conflict within you is out in the open. If you resist the illusion that this is just the other person's problem, you can be blessed with the awareness that you do have a problem and what the nature of it is. You can be shown discernment as to what and how much is yours to heal and how much to let go. This is half the battle. Now you know what to work on.

The resolution of conflicts releases stress, gives you increased mercy, improves your health, frees you to move forward, allows you to receive more without effort, promotes a greater sense of well-being and creates greater clarity, confidence and intimacy. It can lessen fear and give you a greater sense of innocence. This is not a complete list but one that can give you an idea of the benefits of a healing resolution to conflict.

Exercise

Recognize your ability to choose to see conflict situations differently and to commit to the transformation of your perception (which is your projection). Commit to the release of yourself and the others involved from the little piece of hell that every conflict is.

Realize your grievance is just your belief that you know what is going on and what is right in the situation. To presume to know this on all levels of process and unfolding is certainly arrogant. But it is your forgiveness and harmlessness that puts things in their proper perspective and allows you to see clearly.

DAY 30

Any conflict is really a fear of having it all

After about twenty years as a therapist, I began to discover something very interesting happening when we pierced down into the primordial dynamics of people's problems. Many times we would reach a bottom line level where they were creating difficulty because they were afraid to have it all. They would voice different aspects of this fear, such as: 'If I have it all and things are good, then I'll disappear or die', or 'I'll go into melt down and lose my identity in the oneness', or 'If I had it all, what would my family and friends think?!' or 'I can't have it all while so many people are suffering'.

More and more this dynamic began to show itself. Even as we worked down to primordial unconscious fears, many times the fear was actually not of something terrible occurring, but of something totally wonderful occurring. It became clear that people's ultimate fear was the fear of Happiness or of God or of Having It All. To me this was a mind-blowing discovery.

A common fear which people have is that if they are really happy they will lose control. The fear that underlies all the other guilts and fears is not fear of death, as one might imagine, but the fear of life being that good. Somehow the very notion of it makes people uncomfortable, even though it is what they are striving for consciously.

Each problem is a crossroads. It is a choice either to receive a gift or to keep the problem. The gift is a chance to step forward in consciousness, while the problem actually slows down the unfolding process and gives us a modicum of control. I have learned that one of the easiest ways to resolve conflict, no matter how dire it seems, is to receive the gift that life is offering you.

Exercise

Today, begin to examine how you might be using this conflict with others to hold yourself back from something good. Ask yourself what that might be.

Once you have guessed what good thing you might be frightened to have in your life, ask yourself intuitively what frightens you about having this good thing. The answers that come forth pop right out to the subconscious mind. Explore this area as much as you can on your own and then with your partner. If you experience resistance to this concept, do not believe it, but pretend it was true, and examine it yourself and with your partner to see just what you might turn up. It is this that can provide a whole other perspective on your problems.

PSYCHOLOGY OF VISION

Developed by Chuck Spezzano and Lency Spezzano, the Psychology of Vision is a therapeutic model based on relationships, leadership and spirituality. Its key aspects centre about the evolutionary progress, change and the purpose of the individual and humanity. Psychology of Vision is a path of the heart that transcends cultural and religious differences by focusing on that which is essential to human experience.

For further information about other publications and world lectures or seminars contact:

Paul Woolf, International Business Manager,
PO Box 600, Aylesbury, Bucks. HP18 0UL.
Tel: 01296 770122
E-mail: pwoolf@nildram.co.uk

Also by Chuck Spezzano and published by Arthur James

If It Hurts It Isn't Love
Secrets of successful relationships

Chuck Spezzano includes a thought and exercise for each day to help us to look at our lives in new transforming ways, challenging us to open the door to happiness, fulfilment and inner peace.